UNBOUND

T0344631

THE HUGH MACLENNAN POETRY SERIES

Editors: Allan Hepburn and Carolyn Smart

Unbound

GABRIELLE McINTIRE

McGill-Queen's University Press
Montreal & Kingston • London • Chicago

ISBN 978-0-2280-0617-6 (paper)
ISBN 978-0-2280-0754-8 (ePDF)
ISBN 978-0-2280-0753-1 (ePUB)

Legal deposit second quarter 2021
Bibliothèque nationale du Québec

Printed in Canada on acid-free paper that is 100% ancient forest free
(100% post-consumer recycled), processed chlorine free

We acknowledge the support of the Canada Council for the Arts.

Nous remercions le Conseil des arts du Canada de son soutien.

Library and Archives Canada Cataloguing in Publication

Title: Unbound/Gabrielle McIntire.

Names: McIntire, Gabrielle, author.

Series: Hugh MacLennan poetry series.

Description: Series statement: The Hugh MacLennan poetry series |
Poems.

Identifiers: Canadiana (print) 20210158115 | Canadiana (ebook)
20210158417 | ISBN 9780228006176 (softcover) |
ISBN 9780228007531 (PDF) | ISBN 9780228007548 (ePUB)

Classification: LCC PS8625.I525 U43 2021 | DDC C811/.6—dc23

This book was typeset by Marquis Interscript in 9.5/13 Sabon.

for Clara Sophia and Florence Rose

CONTENTS

UNBOUND

MEMORY CHILD

The mollusk shell had left
its mark on a flat limestone shard
my daughter carried to me
in her small hand. "Look,
mama, a fossil. This
used to be a snail."
Together we finger-comb
a caress across tiny ridges,
echo and undulation
where a shell was pressed
to death before we humans
walked or screeched
out art. *The stone*
one kicks with one's boot
will outlast Shakespeare.
"Do you want
to keep it?" I ask. "No,"
and she throws it to splash and sink
beneath a small blue wave,
her voice, soprano's child,
        "Goodbye, snail."

        Her feet leave
dark traces, cup and squelch wet sand.
        Her eyes contain the outside
and us.

What does she remember?
At six her mind is already past
first things, borne thickly with ardor
and ache
for people her heart had loved
who left without goodbyes.
Her own heart's desires:
creatures and magic, contours
of sensation, the beginnings of wisdom.
What's forbidden or impossible.

            I've tried to cradle her to dreaming.

Who can say forever
to her now, and who
can prime her plastic mind
to shapes that twine with hope?

            I remember the feeling
of conception, like the rush and tug
of sudden flight,
the light of her already lit, small
fire.

And the butterfly kicking,
her toes tickling
my insides like laughing
rain. Her first knowing look,
as if, yes, she's been
here before.
"I've come back for my seventh life,"
she tells me. It's a matter
of fact. Nothing unusual.

But this is her favourite life so far
and inside sadness is glory
if you see it right way round,
find the seam, reverse it to perspectivize,
unwind light, joy's unravelling spool,
marking tissue with animal memory
and that same shell on the silted bottom
of a lake's swell.
   Primeval basin dug by a meteor
in its lightening rush to Earth.

  Given some time
it's as if she knows the stone
will shatter and dissolve, too.
To dust return. Given time,
the gift of the unrelenting hand,
we will all meet
in ether and desire. Endless
germination, this beginning
again, always the sense of the new,
the rawness of the patterning,
as if never again,
and never before,
and always the freshness
of the universe's breathing.

SPEED

A pale eastern eagle
        passes,
pressing, presiding,
barely beating
                sky.

Scripting a duel,
        blue-bound, water
whisking.

At war
        with every sluggish
                mouldering thing,
with every darting
                unprotected folly.

At peace
        with ease and chance.

In love
        with speed and glory.

Summer's darling,
        winter's companion,
lone hunter
and catching while she can.

When will *she* lie down to die?
Where do eagles
        speed to spend
their final waking hours?
        One last
sky-nest
        felled,
        and flight their only fancy.

Or, does she
wend her way
carcassless
        straight to fire,
        straight to the eye
                of light?
No way
lost.

BANFF GUEST

"Dear Guest,
Please be advised there has been a cougar
sighting on campus within
the past twenty-four hours."
Elegant letterhead, insignia, art.
Someone in the hallway shouts
"I'm going to fucking frame
that notice and keep it forever."

In the coffeeshop
I ask the woman making sandwiches,
"Did you hear about the cougar?"
"No!"
"Yeah, there's been a sighting."
Searing, joyful eyes scream
across the register. Delight.
The backdrop is snow-capped,
tall windows give
to mountains. Nature is our gallery.
"I hear they weigh up to 180 pounds."

The campus is bereft of travellers.
We take taxis instead of breathing pine
air. Nightwalking is forbidden. Some
of us dream of screeching, clawing, growls.

My cat is curled
back home, unthinking
of the need to hunt.

Someone else had said,
"Did you see the deer? They're by the concert
hall, you might still catch
them. I come every evening
to visit them."

Stepping across a sedge-stained alpine meadow
where yellow-pebbled gorse creeps
to greet a stand of low sitting-stones
like runes signing to the sky
amid a bank of aspen poplars,
I intrude upon their world.

The doe raises tail,
flickers ears when my boot
crunches gravel,
and steps away, untrusting.

Her son
chews grass
and doesn't look up,
but his body speaks:
        "Go away."

I can't help but pass
ten feet from him,
emulating indifference
while quivering at the prodding antlers,
his newly broken skin.

Later I hear more.

"Did you hear a cougar killed a deer?"
Green eyes show wonder like a girl's,
eyeliner and eyeshadow amplifying
as she'd wanted, pulling me toward
distant waves echoing a perfect sky
two thousand miles from here
where a shark fin sweeps
and no one hears the break.

Was this the fawn the cougar took?
Was his the life that fed her?
Those horns won't grow to elegance,
his white tail won't flash in the heat of the rut,
his chest will never fill.

      What wail
does his mother need
to sound,
wordless in
her longing?

      I'd be glad to see a cougar walk by,
right here, to feel his hungry saunter
brush past.
      I'd be gladder if the world were wilder,
if we could let be.

ON BEING CLOSE TO DYING
AT AGE EIGHTY-SEVEN

I can no longer expect to see
the proud, blossom-laden boughs
disdaining the chill
that will at last encase me.

Who could have known
that I would take my leave
at just the coldest, darkest
time of year? Who could have known

the brimming memory-filled regret
for the summer fields and palaces,
and the always endless-seeming promise
of sun-cased days

distilled from time's own pride?
Darkness does not yield,
and my eyes rip at rents in the veil –
tears from the world's own inexorable age.

It is a time of lasts,
and everything is new under the winter sun.
Every gently falling snowdrop,
every band in the sunset's stand of hues –

and each time a soft hand touches my cheek.
I bow, I crouch, I lie low,
and I make myself ready.
Oh, to see another Maytime!

To linger again by the shaded pools,
to go barefoot in the meadow,
and to hear the faraway music
of an unfathomable loveliness.

BREAK THROUGH

The ice broke today
at 11:53 AM, Eastern Standard Time –
suddenly a rivulet
opened up
between the white thighs
of ice.

We had walked on water
just days ago,
confident in the solid support
of ice
thick as coffin stone,
sealed and unemotional.
        A bridge between the mainland
and the islands.

I've been waiting, watching, wondering when
the water's inner boil
would need to break free,
        and it was just so suddenly there
this morning – a blue flat field
of spring calm, winter-framed.
        Blue on white:
deep blue, perfect white.

        Then the field burst a trickle
and a river started creeping
to the shore, meandering,
the sun finally having gotten
through.

I missed it, the happening.
I didn't see the instant of the crack.
Only the darkish shadows
under a thinning surface
hinted this morning
that the breaking point
was near.

It's been nine weeks
since I've seen you,
waters of blue.

      I've missed you, I've anticipated a dream:
Opus 34,
stagione primavera
     in 4/4 time.
Allegro, molto.

LEAVING WORDS

If I wrote for you I would
have to moan first
in animal sounds
against a tugging wind

as if my fur had tousled
with tides that thought
I could not speak
because I had wandered

mutely and too close
to the edges of things:
the points of rocky shores,
the single tracks of cliffs,

the pathways just before
an avalanche hit. I had
discipline and need,
ate only when famished, sang

almost not at all
(and only when the wind was quiet)
pursuing mostly
the wrong kinds of desires.

If I wrote for you it would be on pages
torn from a birch tree in winter, in ink
I'd stolen from the gods –
as if that were more dangerous

than stealing fire.
It would be to refuse
your elegy, watching over you
because the others had left, thinking

you were gone from this world.
But I would see that the smoothness of your skin
still needed licking and attention,
that your hair was still the hair of the living,

not the matted hair of those who belong in the ground.
And I would raise my bright sail of longing
to signal no surrender and no leave-taking.
Only a message, hope-blown.

You would not yet be done,
we would still have need of words,
and I could never be the one
to let you drop away from all things living.

JAGGED

She drew a jagged line
    up and down up
        and down
across the page
    until
        there was no more space

while she listened, or seemed
to listen, her world marking
time like a broken stenographer's
machine.

    In the chair beside her,
        breathing so she could hear
the air between them, he ran
his right-hand thumbnail under
his left-hand thumbnail,
        back and forth,
        back and forth.

    Not cleaning, just
feeling
    flesh
on flesh, the strange
hardness of his nails
like grating shells
against the warm softness
of his aging hand,
himself.

This is safety, a me I know
returning,
        figuring to feel.

        Now I will know
what I have always longed to know,
if only
one more time
        I trace the arc, name
the line,
strike again,
back to the slipping heart
of things.

There, just there.

Like a fish leaping for sun, sky, air,
seeing that on the other side of water
he could grasp, like a wide-mouthed child –
oh! – that line of light,
unsullied.

Pure as first things.

        But lungs not made for this
burn and sear
in reaching for a world
where no fine gauze
kept him apart from the sun
without ever healing
this gash, hook in mouth:
        his unlived and dreaming futures
                before they were broken.

The gasp comes again
        and she hears him breathe.
The nail slips;
the meeting ends.
He wanders to the door.

        She will see him again.

The failure of all goodbyes.

VERMONT BRIDGE

Twenty years later I remember the bridge,
geraniums cascading over
the wooden galley siding, sliding a caress
toward the river you sat beside,
rapids like turquoise ice,
a scene hued by your serenity.

We had nowhere to rush,
not a thing to chide or worry us.
We were so young and thought we had worries,
felt the tug of dread among
the brimming thimbles
of the brooding hours.

But not that day,
not by that river.

We had coursed there
in a borrowed car,
so fancy, fast and nimble
for us, grown used to the limits
of our stridings
as the prime circumference
of available geographies.

We'd accepted that slow crawl
so completely
that the surge into the freedom
of a state map
felt like suddenly singing.

OCTOBER SUMMER

I have come this way
to the whispery-waxy island entreaties
of late-summer cricket songs and blackbirds' play
where golden-brown sun-warmed beauty
today rests, watchful, but reposing:
mellow, under the last true blue sky
of the season's late closing.
Haven for one shimmered, ripple-drawn dragonfly.

I have seen a counterpointed
complimentary purple-ringing flower
set beneath a yellow leaf, anointed
with the too-late summer's fading power,
its conjoinery, its October
bridging the end point of heat and light
with the start of autumn's might,
the opening of yellow, the glowing over.

Flying fast, the cormorants with their black bills
pointed to the heavens, arrows of desire,
mimic this morning's hundred geese in skilled
formation, honking, plucking on the lyre
of the heart's too-taught strings
asking for an unlearning, a tuning
to the never-wearied press of sun and moon
and all things beating out the span of life on wings.

Creature, crouch to our listening
hands that swim
to your lightening limbs.

      Come path-wise, padding
to receive what songs un-furl, un-hurt
time's traces.

      We're *topos* torn
together in this world now.

Firetip moths fly worm-wise
and we humans should forsake
all plans
under this undoing bridge
of our uncomely unbecoming.

Creature, it is we, creators
still, burning to make amends,
standing in kings' clothes when
we should be kneeling

who most need your texture,
whose silent tongues still wait
for the lamp's teachings
written backward.

Stirred up, the muddy earth wanted to speak
of the stores of years it still had in it
in the billions,
forward, backward, not counting

      but perpetually open
to the life it had nurtured and buried,
and all
that it had yet to birth.

But the soundless desire of its inert potential
stayed eyeless in strangled quiet
among the slash and craters left by loggers.
Tire tracks like hardened fossils –

frozen-smeared ghosts of trudge
as wide as the grandest
      felled tree:
an alchemy of earth become dirt.

      The brooks run
clogged with oil
cans, plastic, a stray doll
once loved, coffee cups

from a chain we frequent.
      Crumpled magazines weighted
by ooze and sludge push dirty rainbows
into deadpan pools.

Evening falls serenely on the wastage
calculated in vectors
       and planners' algorithms
              in cities across the grand and gaping world

at desks compacted
from glued wood chips
forced to keep company.
Savings from the clear cuts.

          Those hunters, gatherers knew not so
very long ago
          how to paint treasures on these trees,
          give faces to the quiet. How to borrow,
not steal.
          Only take with blessing and return.

SILVER POINT

"It is difficult
To get the news from poems,"
a great writer said
in another century, dying of love.
"Yet men die miserably every day
For lack
Of what is found there."

You heard that call, ringing through the years
and miles, across the continents' matted
ears that no longer hear
whispers beneath the coding, or
the music beneath the fading
of the languages
we are forgetting as they die.

You bettered the singer's song,
bringing that lyric light
to hands and eyes, shining
something silver (like silver point
in the magician's pen)
not only on our exaltations and catastrophes,
rosès and splendours,
but by saving words that matter,
saving us from ourselves.

If bark, worn off,
  smoothed by sun, wind,
     sky, nights we can
        scarcely imagine, if
bark breaks and drops
to make soil as easily as a fluttering
     breeze
        takes seeds
     from a flower,
        why
can we not lift
     this chest of myrrh, or
one drop of dew,
        heavenward –
           simply to the sky?

SHADOWLAND

Imagine intimate
broken prayers
made to cold stone
vulnerable
to solicitude, a riven
tenderness where
regretful throats at last
forgive the dying
and the dead.

We're not afraid
any longer to return
to our pallid selves
and the end
of the day alone
when the light dims
and gives relief
to rest
within the human-meeting-infinite
chance, accepting
another
magnetism,
drawing us,
exposed (illnesses,
nightmares, obscurities).

I know you
have already

been there
and have words to share
about the place's simplicity
but we are not
surrendering
yet.

EDGEWATER

Old women, soon to receive their lovers,
groan, as if in birth, a first birth, unpreceded
by any unbearable pain or outrage,
having forgotten the memory
inside musculature, within bones
and what clings to them,
having craned enough with crooning,
having outdone themselves
in beauty's pageant before,
but ready.

Old men, soon to receive them,
pant, want, and resist, only
to turn away, figuring
they would do better to bestow
themselves to a scholarly sea,
a tide surging
with the earth's internal remembrance:
another kind of longing
that knows nothing of the flight from past time,
and everything of rhythm, chance, and abundance,
swellings of darkness
                    and the photoelectricity
          of waves of eternity.

          The sea could swallow all of us
without fathoming
                    a misdeed or a loss.

Old women, come dance before the porpoises,
frolic before the ospreys. Strip
yourselves quickly, the moon is rising.
             It is time.

Old men, come sweating from your
altars of sand and loam,
come to these boundaries
of the wine-dark sea
that know how and why
to draw, perpetually,
the line between chaos and order,
beneath and above, water
and the cry of the land,
charting divisions within
the unruled miracle.

The horizon knows you.

             But come only if in the approach
a new enchantment
                    is born.

We sound this naked heart-cleft cry
    together with the lost bones of the world.

  This time-burning fine flame
is ready for anything –
homage, blessing, transformation –
      and not unlike the sea's resolve.

We come, flesh-full,
    opening
    to a pure and perfect
solace, forgetting
while towers
    burn
and collapse,
    not regretting
the stark spectacle.

All will persist, falter, and return,
    the rhythm
    varied
but the force and blush
intact, incandescent
    as our seeking.

We are here. It is
    today. The valley's sun
has risen.

FIRE

You sat with me
under a coven of stars
in a dark but warm
night. The wind touched
your sleeve as you turned
the twigs in the fire.

A DESCRIPTION OF AN APPROACHING
HURRICANE, TORONTO

Do these August crickets know
the fading New Orleans hurricane
on its northern path ascending?
Do these persistent choristers already sign and sing
what we rely on news to tell –
that the hard-ridden eye of the storm
is raging now
through the last of summer's fields, barely
beyond the border, tossing
creatures, cosmos, and late roses aside
in unreasoning and sublime ecstasy?

For, I tell you, every animal knew
the moment of the eclipse on another August day
in the Lakes. The cows bellowed,
the coyotes barked and howled,
every dog in the valley manically hot
with some fine lightning rod
of detection while I sat by
dumbly with my watch, wondering
when it would be,
the exact crescendo of darkness:
the first full-solar eclipse since 1927.
Virginia Woolf had written, "Then –
it was over till 1999. We had fallen."

I was there in that future she imagined, felt
the faint darkness of a lifetime descending.

Now the patter of the rain gathers
in the brightened skirts
of cricket song, past
the city's towers, braced
in a quickly fallen lakeside fog.

The drops – tympani,
sweet rhythm-chime –
make an alternating choir:
        tempest-torn,
but hope still sung.

GARBAGE

What if you had said those things aloud
while the violin note sounded

in the concert hall.
What if we all stopped reading our phones and started
writing letters again and waiting
without waiting
for a response, for days or even weeks?

Like it used to be when
we all had time

before saving time
became our most dignified obsession
and we spun out of control on the time wheel,
forfeiting infinity.

Because you can't hold time

if you're always skimping it,
and that flower that came,
that vase you filled for her in case
she came too, that was in another
world of carrying the weight of me, and you, and us
and all that was.

We're fuller now, but weightless,
so light we might only be

flickers, barely marking the wall,
easy to dispose of:

bright kindling. Garbage for pick up,
treasures for some.

LAKESIDE

The June lake
today is almost
waveless. Azure bright,
fairy-ripple-ridden
with fine sighs, splayed and roused,
heavened by the breath
of some unseen wing
of gravity and grace,
above and below.

IF YOU WOULD PLEASE

(for Gertrude Stein)

If you would please
transfer me to another,
transport me somewhere,
            possibly to the sky.

If you would or could or might,
if you would please
wake me from my slumber
call upon something I have forgotten,
trail your blazing arms across my bosom
the light might fall a little differently,
the sky itself might move a fraction closer,
            the words of everyday might sing again.

If you would please be a you to me,
a one wanting me as another one
wants another one,
a one wanting a you
and a you I could call you
asking you to please
be you to yourself
for me and for you
while I can also be your you,
            the wind might wind its way
                        past ribs, through flesh
to touch those delicate places
where your fingers have also touched,
            in the night.

FANCY

Smear some tongue
swim like rain
chant her forest
and recall skin.

VANCOUVER MOUNTAIN

Canonical mountains frame
this scene
of wayward recollection,
this arena of wish

        sun tides
        the sorrowing moon
        barn owls
        the admonished land.

A film-curtain of pine
needles
                and flickering green

distantly embrace us
with tender
        furrowed
                        reaches.

I was in you all that summer
as though you were a place,
                    crossed the Atlantic
to flee from our unbecoming time.

For two months I swallowed
swollen words, engorged
with a foreign tongue to unlearn
your image, tempted all the time
by better clothes and ancient towers,
eating *gourmandises*,
and frequenting every place, at any time
to put you behind.

And I *was* there,
I know I travelled.
I can recall my poetic address.
        I beheld a partial interpretation
of that mythic city.

But now, when I think of it –
        pleasure
        light
        recovery –
                    I recall nothing but *you*.

In every cornice, gargoyle,
and fountain,
among the hidden laneways,

you embroidered the air,
a sun-ghost shadow above
parched and thirsting summer lawns.

The city's councilors know it needs cleansing,
the *pissoirs* are the street,
and its alleyways leave no room
for the firs, lakes, and mountains
of distant cousins I'd forgotten
in always seeking you.

The magical name:
        syllables stretched taut
                across a still-glowing afterimage

of you connected
        to the fluttering trill of your body.

So like an autumn leaf
        I remember you red

                that December day trembling.

WATERSHED

This is the watershed when no tomorrow comes,
when hope hinged on hope fails to find
the freedom of eager
expectation. This is the watershed,

the treacherous evening,
the night before the years of our existence
in the desert. The night before
the jackals howl and chase

us from safety,
frightening us by the hours that come
and that will never again come. Now is the moment
of necessity, *Ananke*. An end to imperatives

arrives and we can do what we want, but the gift
is less than ever,
a starvation of the soul wrapped
in brown parcel paper, bestowed by a frugal god.

We can't know, and won't,
though fractionally discern that we are facing
an unwanted arrival, a place where
the florid scents that rocked us skyward

and sustained joy
smell of stale paper
and magazines. We can see in this place
that rhythm repeats emptiness, and we will

miss signs and their separation from us. They at least
let our bodies talk. But in this place even leave-taking
is impossible. Divorce from divorce,
meaning without chances to redeem,

nonsense without time to resolve.
This is the watershed where
shadows reflect not identities but dust:
the ash of failures,

final futilities. This is the place
that can no more shed.
Bear no water,
find no flower.

CHAMPS ELYSÉES

I made my way to the Champs Elysées,
playgrounds of whichever gods
we feel we know, and I found
a vast, traffic-snarled
noise-stained
refuse of civilization – a city highway
lined with French-looking trees
and their blankets of dust.
(How does the light get in?
I don't know, but they grow.
Chlorophyll and change happen.)

A few cafés scattered as debris
from the gods' games of dice and chance
cling to the old order –
the old Napoleonic passage between
the Arc de Triomphe and the Tuileries Palace,
selling delicious brews for an amazing price,
a nibble or two for hire,
the sky's the limit
no cheap spenders here –
this might be ambrosia and
these are our Elysian fields.
Here we feel free.

Afterward I wonder,
did I miss it? Was I there?
Is there another Champs Elysées

further along somewhere?
Past the Arc, through
another arrondissement,
just on the other side
of the inverse mirror,
or the fantastic desire
for an outworn spell?

ITHACA

The hills are blue tonight
           and clasp you like a shawl.

Our days want only this
           amicable expanse –

to sail in sheltered shoals,
           to touch cloaked hills.

HUSH

Hush. It's the sound before
there was noise, the silken-slippered
dignity of silence. The wand is pointed
skyward. Fingers touch
woodgrain, bows, keys, air.

This occasion, summoning an aeon
of hesitation, entreats us
to surrender all we came with. Here
is the silence of stars awaiting decision.

                It will begin, but
starting the calamitous chorus,
waiting to be, makes us uncertain of beginnings
and wakings.

Is it rest we want, and not release?

(The silvered silence
                is something we can hold.)

This music casts us open each time
and unmet parts of us remember the notes.

The last time you heard it
your mother was alive. The first time
you sat shaking beside her,
hemmed in, another man's reach
raised, lifting you with the baton,

your father's score the rulebook,
the whole hall hallowed and floating.

Hush-a-bye, she cooed when you were long past lullabies
but hungered for one untangled,
        composed as a sleeping child.

His hand hovers. It's not the time to stop
or turn to the remoter quiet
of distant atmospheres.
The silence is still as it's meant to be
and we are waiting
for eternity pressing
as he lets go.

We kissed by a silver star –
the moon was in your mouth.

FALL

A tender swelling stirs
at the still heart of things
when petals lose
their too-lighted life and fall,
failing at their grasping, all
swoon fading.

I watched, too, the dimming of you,
upbraided by the flinty core
of what we tried
to be, but weren't –
a crystalline idea
carried in our bloodstreams,
forgetting on purpose
that our pockets had holes
big enough to fall through.

Calm was expected,
all bright breezes,
possibly a vernal moon
to coax away a fretting sun.

Tell me, were we bettered
by some mute destiny
who weaves and winds the cloths
of history, or only impatient
with patterns? Does a petal
matter at all hours or only for you
in a deepening darkness where you
hear no fall, regret no lost blush?

THE BLACK-CAPPED CHICKADEE

The black-capped chickadee
      sings my favourite melody:

two notes, two ciphers
      that touch the air and disappear.

Reminding us it's spring
      again, and that springtimes have meant

a sad wanting in the air,
      promises of ecstasy unspent,

roving
      as if being held by the hand

by the one we loved best
      through spectacular warm-weather crowds.

The black-capped chickadee
      every spring sings

the same refrain, offers
      every lover the same

delicate, searching, wondering thing
      sent out through the tops of trees.

But to whom will I sing
      through the treetops this spring,

to what buried idea can I turn
        and again begin to dig?

My own repetition and refrain,
        my own two notes desiring.

AT SEA

From this light-enchanted
    shelf, at sea

                I dreamt of a ship sinking from
                which I needed to salvage
                some of your words.

OUR TIME

Our age, if that is what we call it anymore,
our time, post-post-modern not
post-mortem yet, spreads its anguish,
an uncertain scream.

No mother comes, nor can come to mend
over-chewed circuits –
our craniums like sizzled skies,
our selves cirrus-stretched
and sanded.

This time smiles through a mask
of surprise like the face of the crater-
shaped man-boy in the moon.
We recognize untouchable sunshine
and imagine arriving someplace
quantumly distinct or illuminative,
different this time.

The moon considers her posture,
regales the night,
and promises infinity.

Our time scrapes bone-soul,
makes soup of our blood,
and marinates in marrow, tendon, and gall
as we squat on borrowed land.
This time could be ours, but isn't

because we don't know how to stop
the grasping, touching
faces, those long habits of studying
how to climb into the future
without asking for a map.

The woman upstairs walking
in hard shoes on a hard floor
with no insulation,
the one I've never met,
but whom I imagine
with hair disheveled,
       her kitchen neglected,
       her lover
       gone, and
her mouth set. What name
can I call you?

Or is this heaven tapping, too,
mocking hell's hammered repetition:
a flagrant bid for recognition
from ears forced to bend to this private tale
of drift and paradise ungained,
humility unpracticed? Learning to listen
even when we don't want to. Waiting
for the quiet

       when every rift of stars might skirr homeward,
       Cygnus's northern cross entwining
       entrance to Aquila, Ophiuchus, and Centaurus –
       forgotten Latin tales,
       the end of blazing
       in perpetual rebound
       from the Big Bang.
       A re-arrangement of the universe's heartbeat.

What if I climbed the stairs and found
not her, not a name or a body,
but sound only, pure wanting, a poem
unpracticed, a chanticleer's first crow,
a train's whistle before
– and just after – the release.

A place and a sound unbound?

GIVE

It's so fast, this loss
of wonderment at change this
habituation to losing time, the
present.
       Someone you love
cuts their hair. So
alien, so new, like Christmas
uninvited and then ordinary.

That self gone to the shelf,
given up to the past without saying
goodbye. Strange passing,
one bright candle without

the memory of a match struck,
grey unremembering of black, wrinkled
skin ignorant of the smooth
pebble, narrow eyes meeting the wide-eyed

song of you dreaming still about
the future
       longing.

UNBLOWN

I hadn't looked up, didn't dare to,
in seventeen days, maybe a hundred,
the gift for dates and counting
abandoned long ago
because there really is no time for sky,
or the intimacy of the sky's changes
across a day –
spoils of moonshine, space,
cloud spry and nimble sun.

     No time for the flower
to blow open in a day
or to catch the actual moment
of that hidden falling off
from high summer to the meridian of chill's
persistent return. Darkness drips downside,
and cleaves closer than we remembered.

Time treads on tiptoe,
tripping till she falls outside of time –
no time to lose in the rush
of filling time.
     Time only for memory's snail-
sludge trail, oozing with a brain-filling grief
to stick and slickly stall the future's calling,
snaking pathways, burning highways,
     blotting out the sky's
diamond pavilion.

It's not fair: I've seen
dandelions fracture pavement,
honeysuckle sprays and Queen Anne's Lace
spreading everywhere without needing to know
their names or have a witness,
propagating in lots and fields, droves
of hours in which to ripen,
die, and start again.

CONCEPTION

We've just landed, having
left behind air
for the pull of earth –
a ground I could feel
coming closer with my eyes closed,
gravity grasping us again
as if it needed us.
The distance lessened
in the embrace.

Faster and bigger than any car,
the flight of bright stars
in my stomach: the pull
of you being made, the
tug of longing achieved, the
ache of your beauty
as if it were now.

AFTER A WALK WITH TREES

I

In this place of high trees and moss,
camphor mountains and wild mint,
berries dapple for no one
amidst hedges, the patience
of leaf and balsam.

Here I don't want to speak the words
        of another's tongue with you.

        I will, I know, we always do. What
other words do we have and how
can we invent them as we whisper
words not theirs, but ours, grappling
with scree and slipping stone?
                It's hard to find
a foothold.

The way you think quickens
earth and attachment to symbol;
we worship a churning sky,
dancing us with song,
        like skittering birds preparing
for seed-time.

We both see it, and see it together.
A beginning of things and years
unlooked for,
        ached for.

II

The air is quiet with crickets
and we trace tree-bark,
the chaste childhoods of summer,
fever's clarity. Un-skeining
                    breaks us open.

Nothing need be done.

Earth's ferned touch
scores us to frond the page
two decades later:
        these feet, these hands,
that do not mark, but make.

SPRING TODAY

Pageantries burst in the ravine:
gold-greens, the whatness
of the universe in one sense

every tree like a fountain
(not only willows),
spurting waterfalls,
not shy of celebrations.

                    Spring catches
onlookers between breaths phone calls texts,
the spondees of waking and sleeping.

The trees request attentiveness,
          but so serene
is their appeal without attachment:
          it's not for us – well,
          not all for us.

We find this first gold changed
from other ways and days,
while the sky pities us
and accepts the bloom.

VERGE

I am spooning the sides of your words
to touch what it might feel like to be you.
The press is always side-long, side-ways, a-side

not-quite-striding or strident, but be-side,
as if besides resembled insides.
I'm still so far away from the very of you.

We each imagine fibrous touch lasting
like the solidity of stone, the certainty of beets,
the permanence of atoms –

our bodies more substantial
than the weight of us, sublimer
than the mass of soul,

not evanescent, not always-already
perpetually gone
and disappearing

to brush time and the days
with a wet and wide-stroked swath,
(the finest tip to paint a cloud)

washing across our lives like a dye
that promises permanence, that believes
words matter forever, our conversation,

our churlish language for late children
feeling certain
of storms and the innocence of flowers,

shaping our curvature towards tonight,
today, to you,
believing we are nearer than beside, closer

than the verge of us,
inside, a part. Together whole,
un-rended, belonging.

SPARROW

Traffic snares us. Together we as strangers are
stopped and tightly gridded
between asphalt, horns, and city metal
on the clotted roads.

Through the glare of the spotted dash
a sparrow flits and makes for us,
rising from simplicity, comprehending
time's real pulse, indifferent to our witless
waiting. Needing but never asking.

                 Rising
arrow, veering
at the flash of itself caught
by reflection.

              In a moment gone.

CRINGE

That's how the earth wore you, bent,
crushed by the sky, too,
as if the blue
had always been too
heavy with rain, scent
and chance, but not the chance
of bargaining for few
of these thirty years.

          Not since she'd left,
          the one you'd danced
          and sang with who
          hadn't been the one,
          but became the one
          through time's miscreance.

Kilograms pressed flesh:
your pound, ground to ground
even though you'd wished
for wings and gossamer
and had been long-ago dextrous
on the wind – so light-filled
that they called your disposition
"sunny."

What had happened?
What was always happening?
          A press of days too dangerous to live

because bound
by weary ways and cares
that carved at you
as if you were a personal sculpture,
the chisel unaware
that you still lived
but longed to die.

Your heavy head, bent,
called no more billows from embers
no more eagerness from girls or women
even though you remembered
them wanting you, and bad,
and you sauntering because
you hadn't found a way to care
and sort of never would.
No, not until it was far too late,
and swagger had become hunch,
hunch a cringe at living.

October without leaves –
the shape of trees.

Snow furrows guide these fields
striking fierce contest
with ten thousand golden sinews
that still cling piercingly
to their wild upward motion:
all that grew and breathed torn,
but not keening, not forlorn,
inviting last summer again,
announcing another stark
season of beginning.

We had all been made into frightened lovers,
shocked to expectantly outreach
our hands, and find
a hot wave of wind
rippling beneath deliberately folded wings
that could incite a burdened wanderer
to wakefulness.

This is just what we were called to do –
just that yearning of leaf
for sky – that ardent abiding
beneath the tree blossoming,
already covered in white.

WINTER'S WAITING II

The mute hopefulness
of this isolated winter
field (seen from the window
as the train flashes past) –
somnolent faded yellow
sedge tufts,
not grieving for a minute
all that was lost
a season ago

          tendrils
          fruits
          blossoms
          longings.

Already preparing to burst
invincible again into the rage
of its own spring – a blind
and passionately kinder lust
than the cool winds
and tempestuous gloom
of autumn's disloyal reds, and more
majestic than the valve shut
tight of winter's frozen ground.

Which winter-patient, waiting field, husk-
shorn, its worn and still-paling hues
        flash and flick to fade
against the cold-sun sky
having grasped at green too long

does winter mean
to cover your heart with this time?

Or does winter lean to spring just this way,
finally impatient of the cloven chill,
the hard-knotted ring of winter
insisting on telling time again
         by arriving at the death of the past,
crashing headlong into unforgiving bloom?

ON THE ROSE GARDEN AT UBC

If Zeus chose us a King of the flowers in his mirth,
He would call to the rose, and would royally crown it;
For the rose, ho, the rose! is the grace of the earth,
Is the light of the plants that are growing upon it!

Sappho

The rose petals rose to meet
each passerby a little differently
at the famous garden by the sea.

Small boys, chasing each other, darted
through the arbours,
doubling back on the garden's patterns,
never touching a petal. A seascape labyrinth.
Crete. Icarus's body falling fast. But, first,
freedom and a wide expanse.

A white-haired woman, stately,
fragile but still uninitiated
to display circled twice, reserved,
not wanting to show
her joy, the abandon to admiration.
Her girl's eyes burned, and her
vexed body betrayed the thrill
of the hammered chord
despite herself.

A young woman, hair cropped,
stopped and smelled *two* blossoms

at different ends of the garden:
a measured indulgence,
not to be confused
with outright ecstasy or worship.

I, too, want to walk among the roses
but hesitate, uninvited to the carnival.

Only the boys are unashamed
among the scented branches,
their too-tense pheromones awakening
tides, shaping hemispheres and mind,
elastic in ecstatic motion
that we crave to know again.

SYLVAN SIGNALS AND THE MOON

(After Emily Dickinson)

A world was born – to us –
and carefree stars agreed.
Someone claimed the gift – we
dreamed we'd crown the moon,
and space,
and fashion them our own –

how large the globe, the Earth,
our eyes –
every heart could fill and fill –

till moonbeams blanched her sister –
corals paled – and sylvan pyres sang,
signaling to heaven –
flames aflood –
our wild dolphins gone.

What mire in our hearts
could scull its way through tears –
our animals unfreed –
forced –
tethered to our greed.

Sail farther – planets
Earth's form has wrecked her shell –
our bidding's toll has taken,
her majesty's – purloined.

SMALL HANDS

The breath of stars might perceive,
with nebula and shine
what hands understand with mind –
      the touch of patterning without pattern,
roiling to feel –
      small hands digging earth,
cradling cool, fertile, loaming,
touch-hungry to finger
yesterday's flash of storm,
that grounded energy and frenzy –
the new, bright growth,
      green breaking and wending after
the exclamation of atmosphere.

Amaryllis, star
      flowers, Ipheion. The sky
            itself chasing us
      to summer.

We will never stop
the greening,
because the universe is not entropic
      but expanding, always –

to small hands
      reaching.

ACKNOWLEDGMENTS

I am filled with gratitude as I recall the many people who have offered insight, advice, and encouragement in one form or another as I wrote these poems. I am particularly thankful to Ian Ayres, Brian Bitar, Eduardo Cadava, John Fraser, Elizabeth Greene, Steven Heighton, Linda Hutcheon, Michael Koch, Jodie Medd, Patrick Moran, Kip Pegley, David Reibetanz, Hortense Spillers, Brian Stock, Scott-Morgan Straker, John Sutton, Craig Walker, and the late Patrick Lane. Your words and attentiveness have meant more than you may know.

Kim Ondaatje's Blue Roof Farm poetry gatherings offered a community of poets when I first landed in Kingston. Thank you, Kim, for these memorable readings and hikes together. My time at the Writing Studio at the Banff Centre for the Arts under the mentorship of Greg Hollingshead was a godsend. The guidance there – both formal and informal – of Colin Bernhardt, Stephanie Bolster, John Glenday, Jennifer Glossop, Daphne Marlatt, Don McKay, and Meg Wolitzer was deeply invigorating and sustaining. I also learned so much at Banff from other writers at the Studio and in residence, including David Chariandy, Kelly Drukker, Micheline Maylor, Moira MacDougall, and Lisa Pasold, who have given me invaluable support.

At McGill-Queen's University Press I owe much gratitude to Carolyn Smart, whose work I have admired for years, and to Mark Abley for his inspiring role at the Press and beyond. Allan Hepburn's careful eyes graced every page many times, and he has been the most meticulous and thoughtful editor anyone could dream of having.

I am thankful to the editors and publishers of the journals and collections in which several of these poems have appeared (some in a slightly different form), including *The Literary Review of Canada*, *Freefall*, *The Cortland Review*, *Audeamus*, *Van Gogh's Ear*, *The Original Van Gogh's Ear Anthology*, *The A-Line*, *Kingston Poets' Gallery*, *Remembering Colin: A Gathering of Poems for Colin Bernhardt*, and *Scapes*.

In "Memory Child" the italicized lines are taken from Virginia Woolf's *To the Lighthouse*. I also borrow from William Carlos Williams's "Asphodel, That Greeny Flower" in "Silver Point," and the epigraph to "On the Rose Garden at UBC" comes from a poem attributed to Sappho, usually translated into English as "Song of the Rose."

Xiren Wang and Rupert Lang, you each put poems of mine to musical scores, giving them life in another sphere, and I am honoured. Thank you also to Eliot McIntire for opening my eyes to a scientific appreciation of the natural world, and to Tibra Ali for ongoing and very patient explanations of quantum physics.

I am also grateful to my stepfather, Harley Smyth, for his literary sensibilities and for the writing haven of Amherst Island. The manuscript could not have been completed – or even begun – without the unwavering and generous love and support of my mother, Carolyn McIntire Smyth, who sang me into poetry from the beginning. Great thanks to my father, Thomas McIntire, for nature walks in the city and for his contagious love of languages. Finally, Clara McIntire and Florence McIntire, you bring joy to me every single day and you have been two of the kindest readers I could ever imagine, always asking for "more."